TRAUMA TREATMENT USING

NARRATIVE THERAPY AND THEOLOGICAL REFLECTION

JAMES Y. PENNINGTON

To my wife, Jenny, and my sons, Luke and Nicholas

CONTENTS

The Beginning

We are a story ready to be told. Our stories provide connections. Stories can connect us with parts of ourselves that we do not normally relate to, such as our younger self, traumatic self, or future self. Stories also connect us with other people. Our stories can impact others. Hearing a similar story to mine can take me back to my story with all the emotions that come with it. For example, I heard a Vietnam veteran talking about an event that occurred when he was in Vietnam around Christmastime with local children singing in a chapel. When he recounted how the chapel was attacked, I found myself back in Iraq where our chapel was mortared several times and our dining facility was attacked on December 21, 2004.

This book combines the ideas of writing and incorporating God or spirituality into our traumatic stories to help heal our trauma. This book challenges you to reflect theologically on trauma you may have experienced. Theological reflection is the practice of reflecting on events in your life as related to your Christian faith, and everyday life. This book encourages you to bring your faith and traumatic events together.

Often, we do not see God in the traumatic event unless we intentionally look for his Presence.

Writing is a noninvasive and effective means to treat trauma. The equipment is minimal: pen, paper, and the willingness to write. You can write anywhere. People may write as often as needed. Writing God into the trauma may not bring about complete and immediate healing, but it will be part of the process of healing.

The biblical Fall is the original trauma that people experienced. The Fall is a term used by theologians to describe mankind's first sin and fall from God's grace, resulting in their expulsion from the garden of Eden, sometimes referred to as the original sin (Hoekema, 1996). Theologians debate what happened, but it seems man was no longer the same. Our wholeness or shalom had been distorted. "Shalom is shattered by sin." (Allender & Fann, 2005). Sin has damaged us throughout our being; our bodies, our souls, and our minds suffer from this original trauma. We are broken and no longer whole.

Since that moment of brokenness, it has been God's intent to bring wholeness to humankind. The healing ministry of Christ can be understood against this backdrop.

For example, it seems there was no sharp cleavage between sickness and sin—the former belonging to the body and the latter to the soul—in the classical sense. Concerning the man 'sin of the palsy' He could ask, "Which is easier to say, 'Thy sins be forgiven thee,' or to say, 'Arise, and walk?'" (Matthew 9:5). His ministry was directed to a total need. (Provonsha, 1959).

When people write about their specific trauma, this writing contributes to healing. It is my belief that for those that are religious or spiritual, writing God into their traumatic story is a natural extension of their faith. Often our belief in God creates meaning for us. For readers who may not consider themselves spiritual, I would encourage you to think in terms of writing meaning into your story. The importance of finding meaning is discussed later in the book.

I have personally used writing as a means of healing. I served in Mosul, Iraq in 2004 as an Army chaplain. While I brought a notebook to Iraq with the intent to journal, I did not write every day. I found myself only writing when something significant happened, and writing about that event helped me process it. The deployment lasted twelve months, so there were many events to process.

My most traumatic events included being exposed on the open ground during a mortar attack, having our headquarters building mortared, and having our chapel mortared on Sunday morning while I was in the pulpit, a direct hit that blew the windows out of the chapel. The most traumatic event for me was when a suicide bomber disguised as a friendly Iraqi soldier exploded a vest in our dining facility. The blast killed twenty-two and wounded many more. While the immediate event was traumatic enough, the follow-up with the surviving soldiers started to take a heavy toll on me personally.

I provided counseling for surviving soldiers who were not sent out to a larger medical facility and for those who were directly or indirectly affected by the dining facility bombing. I found the experience starting to affect me. I was exposed to the original trauma, and I was now listening to stories of others who had been exposed to the same trauma. I did not sleep very much. I wandered about my duties like a man in a bad dream. I found myself in a dark place where my stories and the stories of the other people who experienced the bombing began to merge. I had trouble separating what happened to me and what happened to the people I counseled.

The stories were loose fragments, not belonging to a specific time or person, just floating in my head. I started to write to bring order to these fragments and to take ownership of the stories that belonged to me. The effects of the trauma were immediate. The units started holding memorial services for those killed in the bombing. When I walked into the area for the first service, I had a flashback or a panic attack. Our unit physician started me on medication that day. This was the fourth month of my twelve-month deployment. I experienced many of the classic symptoms of being exposed to trauma, such as nightmares, avoiding groups of people, feeling detached and emotionally numb, being easily startled and always on guard, and sleep disturbances.

I also experienced things that seem to be specific to me and my function as a chaplain. Before the chapel attacks and the dining facility bombing, I really enjoyed preaching. After those events, it took great mental energy to preach. I felt exposed on the platform and unable to emotionally connect with myself or others. I wanted to avoid hospitals, memorial services, funerals . . . anything that reminded me of death.

After my assignment in Iraq, I was assigned as a hospital chaplain at Walter Reed Army Medical Center in Washington, D.C. The hospital received many causalities from Iraq and Afghanistan. I was honored to serve in that position for four years. While stationed at the hospital, I was selected to attend doctoral education. I wanted my degree to help the returning soldiers. Remembering my use of writing to deal with my trauma during and after Iraq, I chose to write my dissertation on narrative therapy and theological reflection.

I finished my Doctorate in Ministry degree in 2010 with my dissertation called *Putting The Pieces Together: Narrative Therapy and Theological Reflection.* The writing of the dissertation, the writing of my book, *Mosul,* and the writing of this book have been, in a sense, my attempt to apply the concept of narrative therapy and theological reflection to aid in my own healing process. While I realize this methodology may not work for everyone, I encourage you to be open-minded, because it may work for you.

I believe that God wants people to be healed of their trauma. God wants us to be whole. The journey to wholeness can be understood by the telling of a story or narrative, the trauma that is encountered along the way, the spiritual pain we will feel when we have shattered assumptions because of our trauma, and finding meaning from the trauma.

Many biblical characters illustrate narrative, trauma, shattered assumptions, and meaning. Often, when someone experiences a traumatic event, they feel like their life has shattered. Throughout the book, I will use the life of Joseph to provide insight into how God puts the pieces back together in a person's life.

TRAUMA

Trauma can be complex to define. The word itself is from Greek, meaning a "wound" (Soutis, 2006). The original idea is one is usually wounded in battle. When you are wounded, you are traumatized. This book will use the word trauma to refer to psychological trauma. Trauma may include the physical but it encompasses more than the physical. Since a physical wound has physical pain, perhaps it is helpful to think of trauma as psychological pain. Psychological pain may be defined as a lasting, unsustainable, and unpleasant feeling resulting from a negative appraisal of an inability or deficiency of the self. This negative self-appraisal is typically brought on by the loss of someone or something, or the failure to achieve something that is intimately linked to core psychological needs (Meerwijk and Weiss, 2011).

The closest fitting definition was likely presented by Orbach (2003), who defined mental pain as "a wide range of subjective experiences characterized as an awareness of negative changes in the self and in its functions accompanied by negative feelings" (Orbach, et al., 2003, p. 228). The best trauma interventions will attempt to address all the aspects of trauma. While trauma is defined above as a wound or psychological pain, this definition does not speak to spiritual wounding. Since man has a spiritual component, any interventions must address the spiritual (Liebert, 2019).

In his book, *Myths of Trauma: Why Adversity Does Not Necessarily Make Us Sick*, Joel Paris describes the implications of language creep that results in overdiagnosis of post-traumatic stress disorder (PTSD). Once, trauma meant something happened to me that shifted my worldview or shattered my assumptions of myself, others, or the world. Now it seems to mean something bad happened to me. Since trauma is a criterion for a diagnosis of PTSD, the shift of the definition of trauma to something bad happened has resulted in the overdiagnosis of PTSD. Not everyone who experiences trauma will develop PTSD (Paris, 2023).

The clinical definition of trauma is found in *Diagnostic and Statistical Manual of Mental Disorders* (2013). The definition is taken from post-traumatic stress disorder (PTSD) criteria. The *Diagnostic and Statistical Manual of Mental Disorders* (2013) defines trauma as exposure to actual or threatened death, serious injury, or sexual violence in one (or more) of the following ways:

- Directly experiencing the traumatic event(s).

- Witnessing, in person, the event(s) as it occurred to others.

- Learning that the traumatic event(s) occurred to a close family member or close friend. In cases of the actual or threatened death of a family member or friend, the event(s) must have been violent or accidental.

- Experiencing repeated or extreme exposure to aversive details of the traumatic event(s) (e.g., first responders collecting human remains; police officers repeatedly exposed to details of child abuse). Note: This criterion does not apply to exposure through electronic media, television, movies, or pictures, unless this exposure is work related (American Psychiatric Association, 2013).

The broader definition of trauma is when someone experiences an event that is very upsetting and it temporally overwhelms their internal resources and causes prolonged psychological symptoms (Briere and Scott, 2015).

Trauma can affect every part of the human being. Trauma affects people physically, mentally, relationally, and spiritually. Trauma can cause someone to view the world from a different position—a position of pain and distrust. Trauma changes a person. Metaphorically, a traumatic event causes an individual to lose parts of themselves, like a puzzle missing several pieces so the puzzle is not complete or whole. Without the missing pieces, the puzzle does not make sense. Narrative therapy and theological reflection place the pieces into the puzzle.

If anybody knew about unfair treatment, about mistreatment, and about being an innocent victim on the receiving end, it was Joseph. First, he received unfair treatment from his family. Today, this would be characterized as child abuse, both physical and emotional. His brothers hated him and wanted to kill him but sold him into slavery instead. Next, his circumstances were unexpectedly restricted. He became a slave in a land where he didn't even know the language. One minute he was a seventeen-year-old boy with his whole life before him, and the next he was totally at the mercy of—actually the property of—some stranger.

We don't know how he was affected because the Bible doesn't detail that. However, it is common for people to develop depression, post-traumatic stress syndrome, anxiety, and many possible conditions as a result of physical and psychological trauma. Following all of the above, Joseph was falsely accused. After earning the favor of his master, Potiphar, his master's wife tried to seduce Joseph. As a result of her lies, he was unjustly put in prison and abandoned. His assumptions of how his life should have turned out were shattered.

In my assessment, trauma causes the images of traumatic events to swirl about in a person's mind without beginning or end. Writing reduces the swirling and attempts to put the events in a linear, causal chain. Just as a narrative consists of events in a plot, trauma can damage or break the plotline. Trauma can cause fragmentation. This fragmentation occurs when some integrated aspect of a person's life separates from the rest of their personality and functions independently.

In a case study presented in the article, "The Experience of Time in Acute Psychosis and Schizophrenia," a patient became fragmented because he accepted two separate stories about himself. "These fragments showed that there were two different kinds of stories about the patient ... These two stories carried two different expressions of the structure of the time. The patient was situated in-between these two contradictory stories ... this caused anxiety and disintegration" (Holma & Aaltonen, 1998).

It is my assessment that trauma or PTSD symptoms are a result of being stuck in different structures of time. People may seem to phase through different states of psychological time. The person in the present cannot reconcile what has happened to him or her at the time of trauma. A part of the person, the trauma, is stuck at that moment in the past.

Traumatic experiences often cause four typical stress responses initiated by our sympathetic nervous system: fight, flight, freezing, or fragmentation. The sense of fragmentation is a form of dissociation. Telling the story from start to finish, complete with all the details, is crucial to helping people reverse their dissociation. "The configuration of the plot also imposes the 'sense of an ending'; the events of the story lead to an end" (Holma & Aaltonen, 1998).

Narrative therapy is not a process of differentiating the personality by creating alter egos or "getting rid of" parts of the self which become unwanted; it is a process of integration. "Trauma also disrupts the psychophysiological connections that facilitate story-making. The narrative offers a structure for binding psychophysiological events, that is, affect, with mental events or cognition" (Wigren, 1994).

Psychological trauma is the mind's response to stimuli that present a perceived, overwhelming threat of serious bodily injury, death, or destruction to oneself and/or significant others, loved ones, and those to whom we connect or have a relationship of responsibility. Our core belief system that is essential to our life and well-being, such as, "I am safe," or "God is good," or "the universe works according to rules," is challenged. "In the 'purest' sense, trauma involves exposure to a life-threatening experience" (Baldwin, 2009).

The characteristics of trauma are distinguished by exposure to that which is terrifying, horrifying, and revolting. Trauma is associated with a sense of extreme helplessness to escape or control events, and it engages the body's primal response mechanisms to promote survival. Accordingly, the survival mechanisms of fight, flight, freeze, or fragmentation are displayed. "Traumatic experiences shake the foundations of our beliefs about safety and shatter our assumptions of trust" (Baldwin, 2009).

The following definitions may be helpful. Trauma is any experience that overwhelms one's normal coping mechanisms. PTSD is an experience of persistent memories, flashbacks, nightmares, detachment, or symbolic avoidance that the individual experiences after the traumatic event. Trauma can overrun our psychological defenses, leaving the trauma victim feeling numb and consequently unable to receive meaning from the experience.

A traumatic event, according to Charles E. Figley, who has written extensively on the subject, is an "experience outside the range of usual human experience that would be markedly distressing to almost anyone" (Figley, 1998). It can involve a serious threat to one's life, health, home, and community, or to the life and health of a loved one. It can include witnessing another person being killed or seriously injured. Traumatic events are out-of-the-ordinary experiences, which usually means that people are not adequately prepared for them. For the mind to understand any event, it must assimilate the information. "Assimilation involves incorporating new instances of what is already understood; trauma is alien and cannot be assimilated" (Wigren, 1994). Such events are not easy to prepare for physically, and almost impossible to prepare for emotionally or psychologically.

In addition to the injuries traumatic events can cause to the brain or body are the losses of family members, home, or other important possessions. Typical emotional reactions of fear and anxiety also cause problems. Trauma victims often experience these reactions physiologically as hyper-arousal and hyper-reactivity. Symptoms can include accelerated heart rate, contraction of muscles, alerting and arousal reactions, alterations in mood and emotional states, and nightmares. These symptoms normally last days or months.

In severe cases, symptoms typically include nightmares, re-experiencing the traumatic event, and avoiding anything that might remind one of the events. A common long-term reaction is a sense of profound disillusionment with life, the world, and one's own self. The trauma victim's inner world is shattered because the victim now perceives that deeply held, often-unconscious beliefs are mistakes. Such victims may experience severe depression.

PTSD is a cluster of symptoms. Modern medicine and most therapies treat the symptoms. However, the experience of the trauma that causes the symptoms goes deeper. PTSD is a spiritual wound, a wound to the soul. It is often an individualized experience. People can have the same traumatic experiences, and some may develop PTSD, and some will not. A difference seems to be the ability to make meaning out of the event.

PTSD can be thought of as a memory disease. Traumatic events are continuously filed in one's short-term memory instead of moving to long-term memory.

This short-term filing of the traumatic event keeps the memories fresh, including the sensory and emotional inputs of the event. The brain is trying to make sense of what happened.

The brain has difficulty moving the memories into long-term memory because the event lacks meaning for the person. Without meaning, the traumatic event is a loose collection of images and feelings. However, once the memories have meaning, they are moved into long-term storage, and the traumatic event(s) simply become another bad thing that has happened to us along with the other bad things experiences stored in our memories. Writing about the event and placing God into our story can create this meaning.

Being a caregiver can also be traumatic. Continuous exposure to trauma victims can cause the same kind of symptoms that trauma victims themselves experience. Various authors have come up with diagnostic terms to describe the reality of traumatized caregivers. The terms they use overlap with one another, and yet each points to a different aspect of this reality.

Emotional burnout leaves its victims without energy or drive. It comes from the stresses and hassles of a job. Its effects are cumulative in nature.

Compassion fatigue is a reduction in a caregiver's capacity to maintain interest and empathy with sufferers. It is different from burnout in that it is sudden and acute rather than the gradual wearing down of burnout (Adams et al., 2006).

Vicarious traumatization refers to caregivers experiencing the same symptoms as the trauma victims they work with, such as nightmares, flashbacks to trauma scenes, avoiding things that would remind one of the traumatic events, and heightened irritability.

Secondary traumatic stress is the stress experienced by a person who helps or wants to help a person suffering from trauma (Adams et al., 2006).

People with *secondary traumatic stress disorder* display some of the same symptoms as patients with PTSD, and it is caused by repeated exposure to such patients. Those who have empathy for victims and who listen to the traumatic experiences of sufferers of PTSD (Adams et al., 2006) are often affected by it.

Though the symptoms are similar, there is a marked difference between primary (firsthand) and secondary traumatization. One such difference can be the way doubts occur. The question that often comes to the primary victim of trauma is, "Why me? Why did this happen to me? I am a good person. I did not deserve this. Life is not treating me fairly." The caregiver, however, after caring for many such victims, may ask, "Why *not* me? What makes me think I will never suffer this way? This can happen to anyone at any time." Then, for the secondary as well as the primary victim, the world becomes a scary place, the meaning of life evaporates, and self-doubt becomes the norm. Joseph started as the favorite child with big dreams from God, now he is in a literal mental prison of shattered assumptions.

SHATTERED ASSUMPTIONS

Joseph interpreted the dreams of the king's baker and cupbearer. The baker was going to be killed and the cupbearer would be released from prison. Joseph asked the cupbearer to remember him after his release. He assumed that the cupbearer would speak to the king and have him released. Joseph had done nothing wrong; he had told the truth. He had specifically requested to be remembered, only silence prevailed (Genesis 40:9-23). Joseph's long-awaited hopes were dashed. What does it mean to have shattered assumptions?

In her book entitled *Shattered Assumptions* (Janoff-Bulman, 2010), Janoff-Bulman describes the core beliefs upon which we build our lives. These are assumptions that make it possible for us to feel secure and safe in a world that threatens our existence daily. In a world that is always changing, we need these steadfast ideas to give us stability so that we can take the risks necessary to interact with a dangerous world. They give us the confidence to try new behaviors and to test our limits. These assumptions are necessary for normal functioning.

Traumatic events make the danger that is always present painfully clear. They rob their victims of an essential optimism about life and of confidence in themselves and leave them with a negative view of themselves and the world in which they live. Trauma victims may come to see themselves as helpless persons in a malevolent, meaningless, threatening world.

Normal experiences can be processed because they deal with the familiar. Because of this familiarity, we understand our experiences by extending or recombining existing understandings. "Information or experience that is too discrepant cannot be understood. Since trauma is information that is highly discrepant, it cannot be integrated without major shifts in existing schemata" (Wigren,1994). For trauma victims, the daunting task ahead of them is to rebuild an understanding of the world that integrates the traumatic event by reinterpreting the event, the world, and the self until they develop a new, believable, and relatively nonthreatening system.

Janoff-Bulman describes three long-term effects associated with those who experience traumatic events. These effects are based on three core beliefs that anyone with a reasonably secure childhood holds, beliefs that are usually unconscious but held onto tenaciously. They may change gradually over the course of a person's lifetime through normal processes of aging and life experience. We protect these beliefs, often unconsciously, by interpreting information from life experiences in such a way as to be consistent with these core beliefs or by finding a way to deny or discredit any new information.

A traumatic event, on the other hand, can cause us to reject one or more of our three core beliefs, hence causing extreme anxiety. Janoff-Bulman calls these three beliefs *benevolence, meaning, and self-worth* (Janoff-

Bulman, 2010). The first, benevolence, is the belief that the world is essentially a good place to be, and life's outcomes are usually positive. Further, this belief holds that people are essentially kind, helpful, and caring. A variety of situations, such as when a loved one dies, would challenge this assumption. A common reaction when people become aware of the possibility of such events is to protect themselves by making a distinction between themselves and the rest of the world: "Even if there is evil in the world and trouble comes to others, bad things won't happen to me." Joseph found that people are cruel, his brother, people lie, Potiphar's wife mistreated him, and that life is unfair.

The second core belief, *meaning*, is an implicit faith that life has meaning—that there is a purpose to this world. This belief often holds that people get what they deserve and that one will be rewarded for doing good things. Job is another biblical character who suffered from trauma. Job's "friends" made this assumption: if something terrible happens, the people involved somehow deserved it. The thought that trouble might come in a random manner without any inherent justice can lead to anxiety, depression, and even psychological breakdowns. Many people need to believe they can control their own destinies. They desperately want to believe that they are reasonably safe in this world. Otherwise, they may shut themselves up in their homes in terror and refuse to step outside.

Religious people typically take one step back from this belief. They acknowledge that they do not control the outcomes in life, but they put faith in an all-powerful God who does, a God who rewards the righteous and punishes the wicked. In order to believe that good and bad events come randomly to the righteous and unrighteous, they would have to surrender the very meaning of life as they know it.

In the story of Joseph, the narrator tells us something about life and about our own story. He shows us that life is not predictable. The simple equation "Do good and good will come to you, but do bad and you will pay the price" doesn't hold. It is more accurate to say "Do good or bad, but in either case, disaster awaits" (Allender, 2005).

Joseph had been mistreated and falsely accused, and he was in prison. In fact, according to Genesis 40:15, he was in a dungeon. Joseph was back in the pit again. How did he find meaning? He found meaning in his relationship with God. Twice in Genesis 39:21-23, we find the statement, "The Lord was with Joseph." Joseph began to see the hand of God in his pit experience.

Finally, the core belief of *self-worth* means that, in general, we perceive ourselves as individuals who are "good, culpable, and moral" (Janoff-Bulman, 2010). Of course, we're typically selective in the way we assess our experiences and ourselves. We judge ourselves as good by virtue of the evidence we are willing to acknowledge but deny those things inconsistent with the virtuous assessment. For example, we may acknowledge our own actions when they produce good results, but then find someone else to blame when the results are less favorable. Alternatively, we may accept responsibility for our successes but not our failures. We may conveniently deny the hurt we cause others.

We don't know if Joseph took any responsibility for his earlier actions with his brothers or how being the favorite son affected him. It would seem, at the very least, unwise that he did not notice the effect him speaking of his dreams had on his brothers. Most people apply these tactics, mostly unconsciously. We keep our illusions about ourselves and maintain our view of ourselves as being as good as or better than others.

When we seriously doubt any of these three basic beliefs, we suffer. For many of us, the difficult experiences of life challenge and change these beliefs. We manage to adapt our beliefs to at least some of the new evidence as it unfolds. However, this normally is a gradual change. Rarely do the three core beliefs change very much except in the case of traumatic events. Trauma brings a sudden and serious challenge to one or more of these core beliefs. "The loss of identity causes threat and anxiety" (Holma & Aaltonen, 1998).

When tragedy seriously challenges these core beliefs, the world becomes a terrifying place. Anxiety rises, and depression sets in. After all, if tragedy can strike good people, then no one is safe. When disaster strikes, we come face-to-face with our illusions. Our only two options seem to be to believe that either bad things do happen to good people or that we are not among the good. Either way, the world has suddenly become a dangerous place. It may now seem that good and bad events are random and there is no inherent justice in the universe. Disaster can strike anyone at any time.

We can see the significance of the change trauma requires us to make by comparing it to normal human development. Ken Wilber describes a normal progression in our understanding of the world and ourselves (Wilber, 2007). He says we typically move through a developmental sequence from egocentric to ethnocentric to world-centric. In each increment, we become less egocentric and see life from the larger perspective of others in our group or in the world.

As small children, we understand ourselves from our own perspective. We identify with our body first, then as we mature, with our emotions, and then with our minds. We determine what is good and bad according to what seems good to our bodies, our emotions, or our minds. In the meantime, we also come to identify with groups. Usually, we identify with family first, then community, a religious group, or an ethnic group. Some of us eventually identify with our nation. We adopt the beliefs, values, and *worldview* of the group(s) with which we identify. What we consider good or bad is determined by what is good or bad for our group or nation. We are able to sacrifice our personal desires for the sake of our group or nation.

A smaller percentage of us eventually develop a world-centric perspective that all peoples and nations are equally valued. We now value most that which is good for the world, and we are prepared to sacrifice our own desires and the needs of our group for the larger reality. Our values may now include preserving the global environment, working for world peace, and having compassion for suffering people of the developing world. A very small percentage of us go on to become theocentric (God-centric or Christ-centric). An even smaller percentage develops beyond that stage.

Typically, we move through these levels from egocentric to ethno-centric to world-centric in small increments as our current experiences in life no longer fit our understanding of the world. In each new state, we give up some aspects of our old perspective and some of our previous beliefs in order to adopt new ones. These changes bring a feeling of vulnerability and loss, although minor.

When we are traumatized, however, our ego is bombarded. It cannot cope with the overwhelming requirements for change. We can no longer deal with the reality we face. We have to react, which we do in several ways. We can shut down emotionally. We can turn to an addiction for relief. We can develop an obsession. We can accelerate the rate of development and move more quickly from egocentric to ethnocentric, or from ethnocentric to world-centric. These changes may be so drastic that we feel we are living a whole new life. The old, more egocentric person has died. A new person has been born. We experience ourselves living in a different world because we are acutely aware of things we could not even see before.

In this unseen world we need to realize that we may not know the plans of God, but we can rest in the assurance that God does have a plan. For I know the plans I have for you," declares the LORD, "plans to prosper you and not to harm you, plans to give you hope and a future" (Jeremiah 29:11).

Narrative

A narrative can be defined as a spoken or written account of connected events. These connected events are a story. Being human involves creating meaning and using language to shape personal experiences into narratives (Greenberg, 2021). The Bible is an example of a narrative. Most of the Bible would fall into the genre of narrative, specifically the majority of the Old Testament, the Gospels, and the book of Acts. Christianity finds meaning in the love of God and the finished work of Christ on the cross. Entire books of the Bible address the issue of meaning, primarily from the Wisdom literature. (Jones & Butman, 1991, p. 332) The stories in the Bible have a beginning and end. These stories are written to teach us and to serve as an example for us (Romans 15:4, KJV).

One question that is often asked is whether narrative therapy is the same as journaling. Perhaps, in a broad sense, journaling could be considered narrative therapy. However, I am making a distinction between the two. Journaling for mental health is considered daily writing of your thoughts, emotions, and behaviors based on what you experienced during the day. I am advocating being deliberate and intentional with choosing a traumatic event in your life that you want to write about. If you journal, please continue and use the concepts of narrative therapy and theological reflection to process your trauma.

Narrative therapy will help a person process trauma by changing their story, perhaps from a traumatized victim to a resilient hero. "The idea is that our reality is shaped and organized around the stories that we tell ourselves. The stories we use to tell ourselves about how we act with one another are not about our lives but rather are our lives." (Freedom & Combs, 1996, p.19).

Narrative therapy holds that the accounts of our lives found in our stories or narratives shape our identities. Michael White and his friend and colleague David Epston are primarily responsible for initially developing narrative therapy during the 1970s and 1980s. Their approach gained prominence in North America in 1990 with the publication of their book, *Narrative Means to Therapeutic Ends*, followed by numerous books and articles about previously unmanageable cases of anorexia, ADHD, schizophrenia, and many other problems.

In 2007, White published *Maps of Narrative Practice, a Presentation of Six Kinds of Key Conversations.* Other narrative therapy resources originate from Dulwich Centre in Adelaide, Australia. The Dulwich Centre emphasizes the history of narrative therapy, both distant and more recent, before describing the philosophy and method of narrative therapy. Goldberg and Goldberg (2013) wrote, "White was a caring, dedicated, persistent clinician with a social and political agenda: liberating people from oppressive culturally dominated, problem-saturated stories and helping empower them to reauthor their lives to develop more rewarding and dominant stories and lead more fulfilling lives. Epston, a social worker/family therapist with an interest in anthropology and storytelling, introduced narrative metaphor thinking to White" (p. 400).

Writing links feelings of pain, grief, and loss to an event, and this connection speeds healing. A goal of narrative therapy is for the patient to reconstruct a complete narrative of the traumatic experience. That is, they need to tell the story of their traumas. The word "story" has different associations and understandings for different people. For narrative therapists, stories consist of events, linked in sequence, across time according to a plot.

The creation of a detailed, coherent narrative with a beginning, middle, and end brings together the fragmented images of the trauma. Writing about the trauma causes the writers to think of what happened to them in terms of a plot. The plot of the story has two functions: it configures different events in a meaningful way, and it configures time (Holma & Aaltonen, 1998). The writing of a traumatic narrative establishes or recreates the relationship between the trauma in the past and the present. People live in a world that is experienced and organized as an unfolding story in time (Greenberg, 2021). Narrative counselors believe that people are a

result of their stories and the stories they tell themselves. The stories they tell themselves are often situational. Narrative counselors see people as multistoried. Counseling for narrative therapists consists of having the clients tell their stories with the intent to change their stories.

There is a tradition of healing that uses the written word (Tina) Besley, 2002). The Bible, in a sense, is narrative therapy (Klassen, 2006). In my assessment, the reading of the Bible as narrative, the preaching of the Word, and our individual Bible studies are a form of healing. God uses the Scriptures to change us. Writing and healing are bound together. God has created us to receive and provide information to others through writing; this written information can be a vehicle of change. At the very least, writing God into the situation will change our perspective on the trauma.

The Bible tells us that Christians are God's workmanship. "For we are God's workmanship, created in Christ Jesus to do good works, which God prepared in advance for us to do" (Ephesians 2:10). It is from the word *poiema* (workmanship) that we get poem, a piece of literary workmanship. Like any poem, the words chosen for our poem are deliberately full of meaning and purpose. Before time began, God designed us to be conformed to the image of His Son, Jesus Christ (Rom 8:29). Paul could therefore say to the Philippians, "For I am confident of this very thing, that He who began a good work in you will perfect it until the day of Christ Jesus" (1:6) (Macarthur, 1986). It is in this context of being a piece of literary workmanship that we start our understanding of narrative and trauma. God writes our narrative, and our traumas become a part of that narrative.

It seems that metaphorically, we lose our soul or pieces of our soul through trauma. The search for the soul, the restoration of what has been lost, and the reintegration of what has been lost are at the core of working with trauma (Wirtz, 2014). A substantial and growing body of literature is concerned with the spiritual aspects of recovery from trauma. This is because, in a traumatic event, the spirit has been traumatized. "Whether it is a jagged, raw wound—or a cauterized numb one the outcome is the same: a person in crisis is neither spiritually whole nor connected to their community" (Coughlin, 2004).

At the time of the trauma, a piece of us gets stuck in that time, and we lose that part of ourselves. Writing about the traumatic event helps to process the pain. "Narrative, or storytelling, is the form by which and in which everyday experience is processed. The construction of a narrative is a psychological achievement. Completed narratives 'make sense' of felt experience" (Wigren, 1994). By placing of the event in a sentence through the tense of verbs, we "un-stick" that piece of us that is stuck in time.

Writing about the event allows a survivor of trauma to place that traumatic part into the whole. Writing about the trauma helps people find coherence in the tragedy and rebuild their shattered emotional world. While the context is concerned with journal writing, their statement applies to narrative therapy. In their book *Theological Context for Pastoral Caregiving*, Clements and Stone say, "Putting into words these feelings that overwhelm and the images that terrorize or inspire can give us perspective on what we experience" (Clements & Stone, 2013). Morton Kelsey further states, "It gives space to deal with inner turmoil. We can bring many problems and fears into the open and deal with them face to face in honest combat. In a journal, we can distinguish between friends and foes"(Kelsey, 1980). The storyteller must attempt to embrace the future while acknowledging the past.

If you think of trauma as a tear or a rip in our soul, then narrative therapy is a way to repair the fabric of our soul. This is the position of constructive narrative perspective (CNP) highlights the value of helping victims of trauma develop *healing stories* and accompanying coping processes (Meichenbaum, 2017). According to Cash (2006), who proposes the constructivist narrative perspective, states "Constructing a new narrative and assumptive world that assimilates the traumatic experience is crucial to recovery (p.110)." Cash (2006) refers to this as narrative repair.

Narrative repair works because of human perception. Human perception is often regarded as being influenced by a direct stimulus. It is also affected by memories of arousing experiences that have occurred in the past. Narrative and memory are intimately intertwined (Greenberg, 2021). In the case of any experience, but with specific relevance to traumatic events, the memory is not just a snapshot of what happened, but a complex mix of the actual event and the meaning attributed to it. This complexity remodels cognition, emotion, and behavioral responses to such an extent that the individual may experience significant and constant distress, even though the threat is in the past and no longer exists (Sugita, Hidaka, & Teramoto, 2018).

This leads to the formation of what can be termed as hot and cold memories. The term "cold memories" refers to those memories which are coherent, factual, salient, and organized and do not cause significant distress when recalled by the individual; they may be considered normal memories (Cardoso & Lane, 2016). Cold memories are specific to different events that occurred in an individual's life and are organized in different levels with each level being increasingly specific than the one preceding it, or memories in a plot or timeline (Robjant & Fazel, 2010).

On the other side, "hot memories" are painful, distressing, disorganized, and disconnected from the plain facts of the original episode. A further detrimental characteristic of such memories is the tendency for them to be triggered by a sensory or environmental cue, which consequently activates the individual's fear response to a stimulus that has occurred in the past. They can be considered traumatic memories (Cardoso & Lane, 2016).

The aim of narrative therapy is to reorganize a disordered memory representation against the backdrop of the individual's lifeline, thus enhancing the coding of the declarative autobiographical memory, or cold memories, and giving a temporal and spatial context to traumatic events to place them in a plot or timeline (Robjant & Fazel, 2010). Exposure through writing narratives of the traumatic episodes continues until the individuals' arousal is visibly diminished (Miller & Davis, 2013).

This is why in therapy, trauma narratives are often written several times. This does not mean that the meaning attributed to the traumatic event diminishes, but it is altered in a way that allows the individual to perceive the event and react to its memory in a less distressing manner (Kangaslampi, Garoff, & Peltonen, 2015). This is possible because we use stories for information, relationships, communication, and as a means of self-awareness. The making of stories helps us put our thoughts in order, develop our personhood, and establish meaning and purpose in a chaotic world (Pennington, 2010).

Narrative therapy uses our ability to tell stories to transform us, find meaning, and look at ourselves. Narrative therapy gives a person suffering from trauma permission to move the trauma from within them to the outside world, from internalizing it to externalizing it. The therapy gives the person agency and a sense of control by allowing them to use their own skills to rewrite their experience (Morgan, 2002).

Because stories and narratives help us make sense of our experiences, narrative therapy works for with people suffering from trauma. Narrative therapy is a treatment protocol that allows traumatized people to tell the story of their trauma in their own words. According to narrative therapy, the ability people must tell stories is a way we can find meaning and purpose in our experiences in this world (Morgan, 2002).

Joseph's story in the latter part of Genesis is one of overcoming trauma. Joseph found meaning in his life as he reflected on his experiences. Joseph used theological reflection to see God in his narrative or his life story. The narrative of his life falls neatly into three distinct segments. First, Joseph's birth to the age of seventeen is detailed in chapters 30 through 37 of Genesis (Genesis 30:24-37:2 KJV). During this time, Joseph's family was in transition; everyone was unsettled, on the move. A low-level antagonism was brewing as his family clashed and argued in jealousy and hatred.

This second segment occurs are Joseph reaches young manhood from seventeen to age thirty. It appears his life is out of control. Enslavement, unfair accusation, and imprisonment plague him (Genesis 37:2-41:46) He experiences multiple traumas, and his assumptions about family and justice are shattered.

The last segment is the last eighty years of his life. These are years of prosperity and reward under God's blessing. Following his trials, he had the classic opportunity to get even with his brothers, to ruin them forever, but he refused. Instead, he blessed, protected, and forgave (Genesis 41:46-50;26). He found meaning in what had happened to him.

MEANING

God is not a psychotherapist, except very broadly in the etymological sense that God heals (*therapeuto*) our souls (*psyche*). God heals the soul because He is the One who created the soul. God is not merely the Creator of our life. He is the Author of our life, and he writes each person's life to reveal his divine story. There never has been nor ever will be another life like mine—or like yours—and God writes the story of my life to make something known about himself, the One who wrote me. The same is true of you. Your life and mine not only reveal who we are, but they reveal who God is (Allender, 2005).

As trauma is one point on the timeline of my life, and my life is but one point on God's infinite timeline. God is constantly writing our story. We are not able to read ahead. In fact, we read our story backward to find meaning. We find meaning in what God has already written. In the *Fellowship of the Ring,* Sam says to Frodo: "'I wonder what sort of a tale we've fallen into?' 'I wonder,' replied Frodo. 'But I don't know. And that's the way of a real tale. Take anyone that you're fond of. You may know, or guess, what kind of a tale it is, happy-ending or sad-ending, but the people in it don't know. And you don't want them to" (J R R Tolkien, 2005).

It is not his brothers who sent Joseph to Egypt; it was God. And God had a purpose for it all. We see numerous clues throughout Joseph's narrative indicating this, but now the central character, God, the One ultimately responsible for initiating the plots and subplots of Joseph's life, begins to reveal the divine plan and purpose behind it all.

Extreme trauma may shatter our sense of identity and undermine our beliefs about the meaning of our place in the cosmos (Wirtz, 2014). Often, we see no apparent meaning immediately after a traumatic event. Later, we find theological meaning by reflecting on the presence of God during and after the event.

I want you to write God into your stories. I found this method similar to the work of Fr. Phillip Salois, a Vietnam veteran and Roman Catholic priest. He said, "My work is to help the veteran to find again his or her sacred story. I make deliberate use of the word refounding, because for many, their sacred story was lost on the battlefield. The process of refounding one's sacred story is one of a journey away from an adolescent view of God toward a more mature understanding of faith and God's role in the course of humanity. It begins with helping the veteran to discover where and when the connection was lost. This encounter is a prerequisite to any authentic reconciliation with God as knowledge and understanding must precede forgiveness and reconciliation (Salois,1995).

People have a natural tendency to try to understand and make meaning out of their lives and experiences. "The search for shalom is infused with the fundamental question of meaning . . . The fact that we tell stories that are given meaning by structure implies an awareness that

life is not essentially random" (Allender, 2005). Finding meaning is one of the many God-given attributes that make us human. "The most fundamental aspect of a human social setting is that of meaning" (Krauss, 2015).

Often, after a trauma victim sees death and destruction, he asks the question, why? Searching for possible stories of where God was when these events happened or why God allowed the events to happen allows trauma victims to establish meaning. Seeing the events as meaningful will help answer their *why* questions.

Meanings are the cognitive templates that make up one's view of reality and define events. A Christian's relationship with the Almighty shapes our ability to make meaning. Narrative therapy helps restore meaning, that this world has a purpose.

Christians must allow their spirituality to reauthor their traumatic narratives, thus giving them positive meanings. This spiritual reauthoring is important because a person's spirituality may enhance or hinder healing. A person draws meaning from, or gives meaning to, events and experiences. That is, experiencing starts to make sense as the person performs his or her psychological functioning of translating it into how he or she thinks or feels. It is individuals' subjectivity, or phenomenological world, that forms the very core of meaning originations and evolvement (Krauss, 2015).

People's level of spirituality will influence the meaning they make of events. Choosing to write God into our stories will enhance the healing process. "Meaning-making comes from looking at the situation in a new and unique way" (Petersen et al., 2005). They must make this deliberate act. "People have the freedom to choose meaning." (McArthur,1958).

God sovereignly works all things for His glory and for our good. Yes, all things. And we know that in all things, God works for the good of those who love him, who have been called according to his purpose (Romans 8:28). None of life is insignificant or wasted when lived under the purposeful hand of our loving heavenly Father. I'm convinced that Joseph came to terms with this early in his life, which explains how he was able to take the blows and sufferings that came his way in such abundance. Realizing we operate our lives under the Father's providential care works wonders when the bottom drops out again and again.

They know firsthand the suffering that comes from that stress, from feeling powerless, and they can carry the same symptoms as the traumatized people to whom they minister. Our suffering as caregivers can compromise and even destroy our core beliefs in the goodness and meaningfulness of life. Victor Frankel would say, "When we are no longer able to change a situation . . . we are challenged to change ourselves," and "suffering ceases to be suffering at the moment it finds a meaning" (Frankl, 1984, pp. 116–117).

Our lives can be filled with tragedy. But far more amazing, we live out our stories surrounded by an angelic host and a multitude of stories that put our lives in context and give meaning to our struggles. We must learn to read our passions to know God's heart. And it is during our tragedies, both past and present, that we see how the waters of suffering have cut our terrain and formed the contours of our character. More than anything else, tragedies shape our identity and our character (Allender, 2005).

As a chaplain, I have spent days and nights with the sick, the injured, and the dying. What meaning comes from that experience? What meaning comes when a suicide bomber explodes a vest full of charges in a crowded dining facility? Perhaps one meaning is so that I can identify with those who have suffered and serve them in a deeper, richer way—a connection that cannot be expressed but only understood. As the Scriptures says, "Rejoice with those who rejoice; mourn with those who mourn" (Romans 12:15).

Write your story to understand the depth and significance of what has happened to you, knowing that God is the greatest editor, and He can rewrite your story and use your story to rewrite the story of others. In the next chapter, I offer practical ways to write as an individual. For those who are interested in writing as a group, I make suggestions for using the group process.

We have seen that people the memory or story of those who suffer trauma are often fragmented. The trauma can shatter assumptions about their place in the world. One way to move the fragment back into wholeness is by writing and intentionally adding spirituality into the story to find meaning. After we find meaning, we are on the road to healing. So let us get started.

How to Write

From the outset, the purpose of this book was to examine the process of healing through writing and help trauma victims normalize their traumatic experiences. Normalization, in the form of writing, helps move those who experience trauma toward healing.

The goal of the writing exercise is for people to write about their trauma in the context of theological reflection. Theological reflection is reflecting on our trauma through the lens of faith.

Detailing the trauma provides a starting point to move toward healing. This type of detailed writing develops causal relationships, linking feelings of pain, grief, and loss to an event. The result is increased healing.

Narrative processing reassembles a complete narrative of the traumatic experience. That is, you needed to write the narrative of your traumas. The creation of a detailed coherent narrative with a beginning, middle, and end brings together the fragmented images of the trauma. Telling the story from start to finish, complete with all the details, is crucial to helping people reverse their dissociation. Once these dissociated experiences are identified, I hope the writers will have fewer intrusive, arousal, and avoidant symptoms. Writing the narrative should begin to reestablish or recreate the relationship between the past and present memories of the trauma.

I recommend James Pennebaker's advice regarding how people should write—not with a flowery style but with raw emotion. According to Pennebaker, people need to attach emotion to the event. "People should not edit what they are writing; they shouldn't worry about grammar or punctuation or how things might sound. They simply need to write and see what comes out; and they must write about both the event and the emotions surrounding that event" (Pennebaker, 1997).

Writing as an Individual

Session One: Narrative Therapy

Schedule time to write. I recommend setting aside an hour to write about one traumatic event. Find a time when you are alone and not distracted. Use a space where you feel comfortable and safe. Gather your materials, pen or pencil, and paper. You may prefer to use an electronic device, and that is okay. Please use whatever method works for you. Tips for writing are: Write continuously for at least twenty minutes. Do not worry about spelling or grammar. Write for yourself. Write about a traumatic event. Write only about the events you can handle now (Pennebaker, 1997).

When writing about your trauma, choose one event to write about and stay focused on this one event. Write about an event where you felt your life was threatened. If you had multiple traumas, choose the one that distresses you the most. In the first writing of your trauma, insert as many details as you can remember into the story. Start with when you first realized you were under threat, or you were afraid. Use your five senses as a guideline to describe the event. Write about what you saw, including colors and shapes. Write about what you heard. Write about what you smelled. Write about what you tasted. Write about what you touched. Write about what you were feeling. When you write about a traumatic event, what emotions come up for you?

Session Two: Theological Reflection

Schedule time to write. I recommend setting aside an hour to write about one traumatic event. Find a time when you are alone and not distracted. Use a space where you feel comfortable and safe. Gather your materials, pen or pencil, and paper. You may prefer to use an electronic device, which is okay. Please use whatever method works for you. Tips for writing are: Write continuously for at least twenty minutes. Do not worry about spelling or grammar. Write for yourself. Write about a traumatic event. Write only about the events you can handle now (Pennebaker, 1997).

The purpose of session two is to write God into the traumatic narrative. Using the last narrative as a reference point, on a separate sheet of paper, rewrite the narrative with theological statements in mind. These statements are: Describe how the trauma caused you to experience God. Explain how the trauma has affected your relationship with God. When you look back on your trauma, can you see something different concerning God's perspective on the situation? When you write God into your trauma story, you may find yourself angry with Him. This is perfectly fine and normal. Write about your anger and how it affects your trauma and your view of God.

These questions are a reference; the point is to write God into the trauma. I want you to see alternate ways God was/is involved in your life/trauma.

Session Two: Alternative Writing: Writing Meaning into your Story

For readers who are not spiritually inclined, an alternate method is to write meaning into your trauma story. Schedule time to write. I recommend setting aside an hour to write meaning into your story. Find a time when you are alone and not distracted. Use a space where you feel comfortable and safe. Gather your materials, pen or pencil, and paper. You may prefer to use an electronic device, and that is okay. Tips for writing are: Write continuously for at least twenty minutes. Do not worry about spelling or grammar. Write for yourself. Write about a traumatic event. Write only about the events you can handle now (Pennebaker, 1997).

The purpose of this writing is to write meaning into the traumatic narrative. Using your trauma narrative as a reference point, on a separate sheet of paper, rewrite the narrative with meaning statements in mind. The statements are: Describe how the trauma caused you to experience the world. Explain how the trauma has affected your relationship with people. When you look back on your trauma through the lens of meaning, can you reappraise what happened? Describe what your trauma means.

Session Three:
Integration of Narrative Therapy and Theological Reflection

Schedule time to write. I recommend setting aside an hour aside to integrate narrative therapy and theological reflection. Find a time when you are alone and not distracted. Use a space where you feel comfortable and safe. Gather your materials, pen or pencil, and paper. You may prefer to use an electronic device, and that is okay. Tips for writing are: Write continuously for at least twenty minutes. Do not worry about spelling or grammar. Write for yourself. Write about a traumatic event. Write only about the events you can handle now (Pennebaker, 1997).

The purpose of the final writing is to integrate the two previous documents. Please review the two previous documents. In this session, you are integrating the details of the trauma with writing God into the trauma. Write a narrative integrating the details of your traumatic experiences, reflecting theologically, and writing God into your trauma with the purpose of bringing wholeness by retelling the story with God. This begins the process of becoming whole, and this awareness of wholeness will help you move further down the road toward healing.

Writing as a Group

Group Format for Workshop

For those who would like to develop or write in a group, a small group format provides an excellent environment for processing trauma. I suggest doing the workshop as a small group so each participant works through the subject matter themselves as opposed to being a passive listener in a seminar or lecture-based format. The small group format is suitable for an adult to process their trauma.

According to Neal McBride, four basic types of small groups lend themselves to different applications and adaptations:

1. Relationships (or process) groups: The focus is on group processes to establish and nurture interpersonal relationships among the members as brothers and sisters in Christ. Groups in this category are often called "growth groups," "caring groups," "fellowship groups," "covenant groups," or something similar.

2. Content groups: The primary purpose of these groups is to learn and discuss information—

usually the Word of God, but not always. A relationship amongst the members is important but secondary to covering and understanding the material. Many Bible studies and discussion groups fall into this category.

3. Task groups: The central focus is on doing something (a job or responsibility) together as a group, usually some ministry. The group's defined task creates the purpose of the meeting. Task groups include most committees or planning groups, and even evangelism groups.

4. Need-based groups: The basic purpose is to provide support for fellow group members who have experienced or are experiencing the same or similar need. Recovery groups, support groups, self-help groups, and group counseling are all good examples (McBride, 1997).

The writing workshop I designed is most like the task group described above but also includes elements of the other types of small groups. Stating the purpose of the small group workshop gives the group intentionality and direction. The primary purpose of the workshop is to assist people in writing about their trauma and processing their trauma through theological reflection.

Conducting the Small Group

The suggested format is for those who want to participate to meet for a three-hour workshop at a time of their choosing. The three-hour workshop is divided into three one-hour sessions. I recommend that a minister or counselor be present to serve as a facilitator of the group and encourage participants to interact with the subject material.

Each session in the writing workshop focuses on a different aspect of writing God into their trauma. The purpose of session one is to help the participants understand narrative therapy and is concerned with capturing the details of the traumatic event. The second session focuses on theological reflection, the participants, and their interaction with the theological questions. The third session integrates narrative therapy and theological reflection by combining the details presented in the narrative therapy document with the answers to the questions asked during the theological reflection session.

Session One: Narrative Therapy

Each lesson should begin with a disclaimer that no one will judge or label participants in the class. Ask the group to covenant to keep the shared information sacred and not to discuss it outside the group. Give several guidelines for writing narratives. These guidelines are modifications of those articulated by James W. Pennebaker, the Bush Professor of Liberal Arts and the Departmental Chair in the Psychology Department at the University of Texas at Austin. His writing tips are: Write continuously for at least twenty minutes. Do not worry about spelling or grammar. Write for yourself. Write about a traumatic event. Write only about the events you can handle now.

Emphasize the necessity of writing the details of the traumatic event and the emotions surrounding the details. Then, give time for clarification and discussion. This part of the class should take approximately twenty minutes.

Next, instruct those participating to write a narrative about their traumatic experiences, concentrating on the details and emotions. Provide pencils and paper, and allow twenty minutes for the writing. During the writing, it would be a good idea to circulate around the class to address questions.

The last twenty minutes are for the group to share their stories. I highly encourage the sharing of their stories but do not require it. When someone shares their story, there should be no questions or discussion.

Session Two: Theological Reflection

The purpose of session two is to write God into the traumatic narrative. Reiterate the disclaimer that the participants should not be judged or labeled for attending the group. The group will follow the same writing guidelines presented in session one.

During the second lesson, the concept of theological reflection is introduced to the group. The group should use their last narrative as a reference point, and on a separate sheet of paper, rewrite the narrative with theological statements in mind. The statements are: Describe how the trauma caused you to experience God. Explain how the trauma has affected your relationship with God. When you look back on your trauma, can you see something different concerning God's perspective on the situation? Explain that the participants should use these questions as a reference; the point is to write God into the trauma. Encourage them to see alternate ways God was/is involved in their life/trauma. Then, ask for questions and give time for clarification and discussion. The first part of the class should take approximately twenty minutes.

Next, participants should write a narrative about their traumatic experiences, reflecting theologically and writing God into their trauma. Allow twenty minutes for the writing. As before, circulate through the class to address questions, and provide pencils and paper. Follow the same protocol as the first session.

The group should end with a review of the topic and encouragement for those who engaged in their writing. This is also an opportunity for the minister or counselor to offer ministry if anyone needs to talk about what happened. Ask the class to use their narratives for the next class. For each class, the previous topic should be discussed and related to the new topic for continuity.

Session Three:
Integration of Narrative Therapy and Theological Reflection

The final lesson integrates the two previous lessons. As with the previous sessions, begin with a disclaimer and a description of the writing guidelines. Introduce the concept of theological reflection using narrative therapy. Ask the group to review their two previous documents and explain that in this session, they will integrate the details of their trauma with writing God into the trauma. Encourage the group that by retelling their story with God, they will begin the process of becoming whole, and this awareness of wholeness will help them move further down the road toward healing.

Use the same writing guidelines and protocols from the previous sessions. Next, instruct them to write a narrative integrating the details of their traumatic experiences, reflecting theologically, and writing God into their trauma with the purpose of bringing wholeness. During the final session, there should be a group discussion where participants are allowed to describe their experience as a measure of wholeness or healing.

Conclusion

The underlying premise of this writing exercise is that God is actively at work in the world today as He heals people through different means. One of these means is by telling one's story and ensuring that God is present in the story.

When we have experienced trauma, it is helpful to have the mindset of Joseph to guide us on our healing journey—realizing trauma intended to cause harm, but God intended it for good. Because you went through that traumatic experience, God can use you to minister to many people. The story of your healing can be summed up with this insight from the narrative of Joseph's life." You intended to harm me, but God intended it for good to accomplish what is now being done, the saving of many lives" (Genesis 50:20).

In his book, *Soul Medicine* (2023), Ed Tick relates a story of someone healing from trauma emerging from decades of shame and a dark night of the soul, who says, "I feel like I am gathering the lost puzzles pieces of my life and finally putting them together into a coherent picture." I like the puzzle metaphor for healing from trauma. A jigsaw puzzle itself, the cardboard-and-paper collection of differently shaped and colored pieces, is a physical metaphor. You start, of course, with a large pile of randomized pieces. It looks hopeless. Disorder and chaos reign. We know that God wants us to become whole, like the picture on the box. Trauma has broken our "whole" picture; now we just have pieces. Some parts of the puzzle may be complete; they just need to be integrated into the larger puzzle. Others are seemingly just random pieces, and we do not know where to place them.

Is this an accurate metaphor for our situation when faced with puzzles of trauma? Sometimes, yes. We often have a general sense that we are not complete or whole. We don't have the complete picture filled in yet. Writing or narrative therapy is the process of finding the right pieces.

Our conceptual boundaries are like the straight-line borders of our puzzle. We understand certain concepts up to a limit. That limit is the edge of our puzzle. For example, we know, as Christians, that God is in our circumstances, and we need to experience Him in our trauma. We can accomplish this by writing our trauma and placing God into our traumatic experiences.

Therefore, we work from the edges of our puzzle. As we do, certain outlines appear, and we search for pieces that will fit them. We work from the context and try to fill in the blanks. This might be analogous to finding a bunch of pieces that are the same color and obviously belong together. We put them together into a brown building. The resulting portion of the puzzle is then a "sub-assembly" ready to be "plugged in" at the appropriate place as the puzzle takes shape. But the main action is working in, bit by bit, from the edges. Healing from trauma is a similar process.

Early in the puzzle-solving process, there are many pieces lying around. Our job is to classify them and group them together. We must discover what is missing, and slowly, patiently, we move from disorder to different stages of order, from randomness to regularity. The frame is put together. Certain prominent "subassemblies" get assembled. It is interesting to watch as individual pieces disappear when they are fit into place. Similarly, as we process our trauma, the piece of us that was removed from us by trauma becomes a part of the whole picture and we become healthy again.

We continue putting the pieces together until we have the whole picture, which is a metaphor of us being healed. We may not be immediately healed, but we know it is a process, and we keep putting the pieces together to bring us closer to our goal of wholeness. It is my hope and prayer that this book will inspire those who have been traumatized to seek a greater degree of healing by treating trauma with narrative therapy and theological reflection.

REFERENCE

Adams, R. E., Boscarino, J. A., & Figley, C. R. (2006). "Compassion fatigue and psychological distress among social workers: A validation study." American Journal of Orthopsychiatry, 76(1), 103–108. https://doi.org/10.1037/0002-9432.76.1.103

Allender, D. B., & Fann, L. K. (2005). To be told. know your story, Shape your future. WaterBrook Press.

Baldwin, David "About Trauma," Trauma Pages, http://www.trauma-pages.com/ (accessed February 16, 2009).

(Tina) Besley, A. C. (2002). "Foucault and the Turn to Narrative Therapy." British Journal of Guidance & Counselling, 30(2), 125–143. https://doi.org/10.1080/03069880220128010

Briere, J. N., & Scott, C. (2015). Principles of Trauma Therapy: DSM-5 Update (2nd ed.). Thousand Oaks, CA: Sage Publications. ISBN: 9781483351247

Cardoso, J. B., & Lane, L. B. (2016). "Practice with Immigrant and Refugee Children and Families in the Mental Health System." Immigrant and Refugee Children and Families. doi:10.7312/dett17284-01

Cash, A., (2006). Wiley Concise Guides to Mental Health. Hobucken, N.J.: John Wiley & Sons

Clements, W. M., & Stone, H. W. (2013). Theological Context for Pastoral Caregiving. Routledge.

Coughlin, K. (2004). We Don't Leave Our Wounded on the Battlefield /www.vietnamministers.org/coughlin_paper htm

Diagnostic and Statistical Manual of Mental Disorders (5th Ed). (2013). Washington DC: American Psychiatric Association.

Freedman, J., & Combs, G. (1996). Narrative Therapy: the Social Construction of Preferred Realities. Norton

Figley, Charles. Burnout in Families: The Systematic Costs of Caring. Boca Raton: CRC Press,1998.

Frankl , V. E. (1984). Man's Search for Meaning: An Introduction to Logotherapy () , 3rd ed.. New York , NY : Simon & Schuster.

Goldberg, H. & Goldberg, I. (2013). Family Therapy: An Overview. Belmont: CA. BrooksCole; Cengage Learning.

Greenberg, L. S. (2021). Changing Emotion with Emotion: A Practitioner's Guide. American Psychological Association.

Janoff-Bulman, R. (2010). Shattered Assumptions: Towards a New Psychology of Trauma. Simon And Schuster.

Jones, S. L., & Butman, R. E. (1991). Modern Psychotherapies: A Comprehensive Christian Appraisal. Downers Grove, Ill: InterVarsity Press

J R R Tolkien. (2005). The Lord of the Rings: Trilogy. Houghton Mifflin.

Klassen, P. E. (2006). "Textual Healing: Mainstream Protestants and the Therapeutic Text, 1900–1925." Church History, 75(4), 809–848. https://doi.org/10.1017/s0009640700111849

Kangaslampi, S., Garoff, F., & Peltonen, K. (2015). "Narrative Exposure Therapy for Immigrant Children Traumatized by War: Study Protocol for a Randomized Controlled Trial of Effectiveness and Mechanisms of Change." BMC Psychiatry, 15(1). doi:10.1186/s12888-015-0520-z

Krauss, S. (2015). "Research Paradigms and Meaning Making: A Primer." The Qualitative Report, 10(4). https://doi.org/10.46743/2160-3715/2005.1831

Liebert, E. A. (2019). "Accessible Spiritual Practices to Aid in Recovery from Moral Injury. Pastoral Psychology, 68(1), 41-57. Doi:10.1007/s11089-018-0825-1

Hoekema, A. A. (1996). Created in God's Image. William. B. Eerdmans Publishing Company.

Holma, J., Aaltonen, J. "The Experience of Time in Acute Psychosis and Schizophrenia." Contemporary Family Therapy 20, 265–276 (1998). https://doi.org/10.1023/A:1022408727490

Macarthur, J. (1986). Ephesians. Moody Press

McArthur, H. (1958). "The Necessity of Choice [Review of The Necessity of Choice]. Journal of Individual Psychology, 14, 153–157.

Mcbride, N. (1997). How to Have Great Small Group Meetings: Dozens of iIdeas You Can Use Right Now. Navpress

Meichenbaum, D. (2017). "A Constructive Narrative Perspective on Trauma and Resilience: The role of Cognitive and Affective Processes." In S. N. Gold (Ed.), APA Handbook of Trauma Psychology: Foundations in Knowledge (pp. 429–442). American Psychological Association. https://doi.org/10.1037/0000019-022

Meerwijk, E. L., & Weiss, S. J. (2011). "Toward a Unifying Definition of Psychological Pain. Journal of Loss and Trauma, 16(5), 402-412.http://dx.doi.org/10.1080/15325024.2011.572044

Morgan, A. (2000). What Is Narrative Therapy?: An Easy-to-Read Introduction. Dulwich Centre Publications

Orbach, I. , Mikulincer , M. , Sirota , P. , & Gilboa-Schechtman , E. (2003). "Mental Pain: A Multidimensional Pperationalization and Definition. Suicide and Life Threatening Behavior, 33, 219 – 230

Paris, J. (2023). Myths of Trauma.

Pennebaker, J. (1997). Opening Up: The Healing Power of Expression Emotions. Guilford Press.

Pennington, James, "Putting the Pieces Together: Narrative Therapy and Theological Reflection" (2010). Tren Dissertations. 8592. https://place.asburyseminary.edu/trendissertations/8592

Petersen, S., Bull, C., Propst, O., Dettinger, S., & Detwiler, L. (2005). "Narrative Therapy to Prevent Illness-Related Stress Disorder." Journal of Counseling & Development, 83(1), 41–47. https://doi.org/10.1002/j.1556-6678.2005.tb00578.x

Provonsha, J. (1959). "The Healing Christ" [Review of The Healing Christ]. Current Medical Digest, 328.

Robjant, K., & Fazel, M. (2010). "The Emerging Evidence for Narrative Exposure Therapy: A Review." Clinical Psychology Review, 30(8), 1030-1039. doi:10.1016/j.cpr.2010.07.004

Salois, P. (1995). "Spiritual Healing and PTSD" [Review of Spiritual Healing and PTSD]. NCP Clinical Quarterly, 5(1). http://www.ncptsd.org/publications/cq/v5n1/salois.html

Soutis, M. (2006). "Ancient Greek Terminology in Pediatric Surgery: About the Word Meaning." Journal of Pediatric Surgery, 41(7), 1302-1308. doi:10.1016/j.jpedsurg.2006.03.011

Sugita, Y., Hidaka, S., & Teramoto, W. (2018). "Visual Percepts Modify Iconic Memory in Humans. Scientific Reports, 8(1). https://doi.org/10.1038/s41598-018-31601-4

Tick, E. (2023). Soul Medicine. Inner Traditions.

Wilber, K. (2007). Integral Spirituality. Shambhala Publications.

Wigren, J. (1994). "Narrative Completion in the Treatment of Trauma. Psychotherapy: Theory, Research, Practice, Training, 31(3), 415–423. https://doi.org/10.1037/0033-3204.31.3.415

Wirtz, U. (2014). Trauma and Beyond: The Mystery of Transformation. Spring Journal, Inc.

www.ingramcontent.com/pod-product-compliance
Lightning Source LLC
Chambersburg PA
CBHW020358290526
45785CB00005B/2345